MAKING A VICTORIAN
DOLLS' HOUSE

JEAN GREENHOWE

Making a Victorian Dolls' House

B T BATSFORD LTD *LONDON*

© Jean Greenhowe 1978
First published 1978

ISBN 0 7134 0870 7

Filmset by Keyspools Ltd, Golborne, Lancs
Printed in Great Britain by
Cox & Wyman Ltd, Fakenham
for the publishers B T Batsford Ltd
4 Fitzhardinge Street London W1H 0AH

Contents

Introduction

Victorian dolls' houses and their furnishings have become much-sought-after collector's items in recent years and consequently they can be quite expensive. For those who cannot afford the luxury of a genuine antique house, this book describes how a most attractive reproduction can be made from an ordinary cardboard box and other household items.

At the beginning of the book there are diagrams and instructions showing how to reinforce and strengthen the box to make it rigid and strong. The divisions for walls, floors and ceilings are then constructed, while at the same time applying the wall and floor coverings. The miniature house described in detail in this section has three floors with a room on each floor. It is designed to be either free-standing or hung on a wall as a display piece in the way that many Victorian dolls' houses were. Once the techniques for reinforcing and making floors and ceilings are known, then various sizes or shapes of boxes can be utilized to make houses with any number of rooms.

The next few chapters deal with the furnishings of a Victorian house. This is perhaps the most exciting and absorbing part for the dolls' house maker, since the most ordinary everyday odds and ends can be transformed into delightful miniature ornaments and furnishings. Because the house and accessories are made to the same scale as a wide range of commercially manufactured dolls' house furniture, suggestions are given here for re-painting such items to give the desired 'antique' finish.

The inhabitants of the house, family, servants and pets, are not forgotten and there are details and ideas for making these also. Instructions are given for two types of doll. The first and simplest method uses a wooden clothes peg for the basic doll, and the second method shows how to make a more flexible figure from pipe cleaners with a wooden bead for the head.

Next there are suggestions for making a simple open room with only a floor and three walls. This is shown furnished as a milliner's shop of the 1890s, complete with a colourful array of pretty hats. Complete instructions for making a market stall follow, plus details of how to set out the stall with country produce or fabrics and trimmings.

Finally ideas are given for making a peg doll dressed as a street vendor, this being the simplest way of displaying a selection of miniature items for sale.

The Three-roomed Dolls' House

Materials required for making the house

Cardboard grocery box and cardboard
The box used for the house illustrated is about 42 cm (16½ in.) high, 19 cm (7½ in.) wide and 14 cm (5½ in.) in depth. Boxes of this (or a similar) size can be obtained from grocery stores or supermarkets. A few other grocery boxes are required for cutting up, to reinforce the box and for the front opening part of the house. Note that in the instructions throughout the book, this corrugated reinforced type of cardboard will always be referred to as 'cardboard'.

Plain strong card
This is required for the window frames, front door, walls and floors. It should be plain card and not the corrugated reinforced grocery-box kind. Good household sources for plain card are shirt and gift boxes or chocolate boxes. It can also be obtained in different thicknesses from art and craft shops. Several layers of thin card can be glued together if necessary, to obtain the required thickness. Note that in the instructions throughout the book, this type of plain card will always be referred to as 'card'.

2

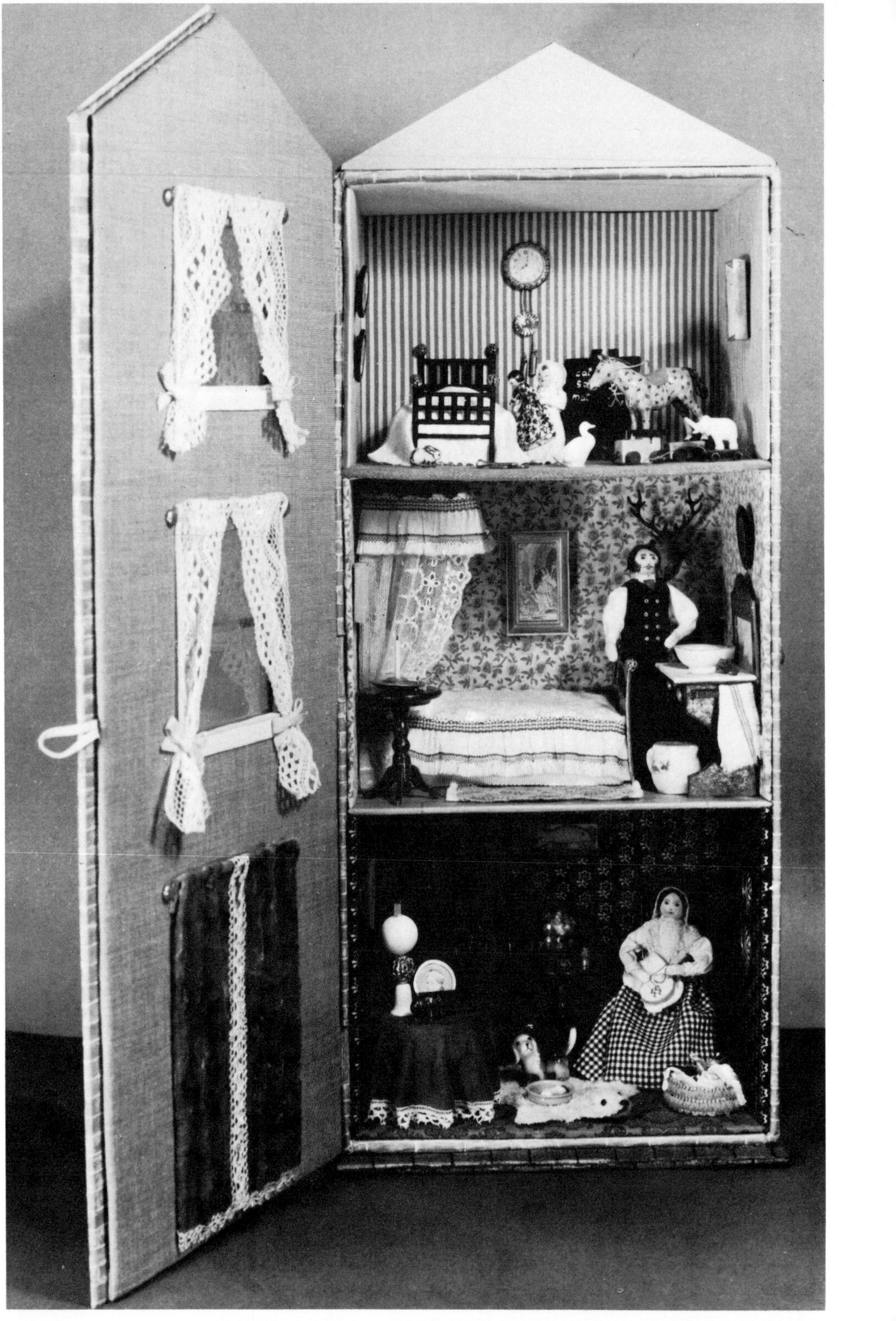

Brick and slate paper
Dolls' house brick and slate paper can usually be obtained from art and craft shops in sheets measuring about 51 cm by 76 cm (20 in. by 30 in.). Two sheets of brick and one sheet of slate paper are required.

Clear acetate film
Pieces of clear acetate film for the windows can be found on gift boxes, shirt boxes etc. (See the list of suppliers at the end of the book in case of difficulty in locating any of these items.)

Wall and floor coverings
Fabrics or paper printed with very small patterns should be used. Fabric is probably the most suitable material for the walls as well as the floors since it is available in a range of very small Victorian-style prints, whereas paper printed with suitable small designs is more difficult to obtain. See chapter 3 for further ideas before starting to cover the walls and floors.

Other materials required

Seven brass paper fasteners

Small length of narrow elastic

A D-ring and piece of strong ribbon for the hanging loop at the back of the house

Petersham ribbon, 24 cm ($9\frac{1}{2}$ in.) long by 2.5 cm (1 in.) wide, for the hinges on the front face of the house

Small button for the door knob

Scrap of junk jewellery for the door knocker

Enamel paint for the door and window frames

Quick-drying adhesive (such as all-purpose UHU glue)

Craft knife and strong scissors for cutting the cardboard

Ruler, pencil and tape measure

A steel rule, if available, is especially useful as a firm guide when cutting straight strips of card with a craft knife

To make the house
The flaps on the base of the box should be firmly stuck down. If they are at all loose, pull them apart and stick again. Turn the remaining top flaps to the inside of the box and stick them down. These flaps will serve to strengthen the box, but they may not be deep enough to completely cover the inner sides. Cut narrow strips of cardboard off the spare grocery boxes to fit these areas and glue them in place alongside the flaps, as indicated in diagram 1.

The hanging loop, if required, should be stuck to the back of the box next. Slip the length of strong ribbon through the D-ring and stick the ribbon to the box back as shown in diagram 2. Now reinforce the entire back of the box by gluing on a rectangle of card cut to fit.

Now cut a strip of brick paper to go round the sides and back of the box adding 2 cm ($\frac{3}{4}$ in.) extra to the strip all round. Stick the brick paper in place, turning and gluing the 2 cm ($\frac{3}{4}$ in.) extra to the inside of the box at the front edges, and onto the top and base of the box. Stick on rectangles of brick paper to fit the top and base of the box, adding 2 cm ($\frac{3}{4}$ in.) extra at the front edge to turn to the inside of the box in the same way as for the sides.

Cut the petersham ribbon into three equal lengths. Stick half of each piece of ribbon to the inside left-hand wall of the box for the hinges, as shown in diagram 3.

To allow the front face of the house to swing open properly, a small section of the wall behind each ribbon strip must be cut away. Cut a recess about 5 mm ($\frac{1}{4}$ in.) deep in the edge of the wall behind each ribbon strip as shown in diagram 4 using a craft knife. Neaten the cut edges of these recesses by sticking on small patches of brick paper.

When closed, the front face of the house is held in position by a loop of elastic fixed round a paper fastener, which is embedded in the wall of the house opposite the hinges. Push the paper fastener through the wall as shown in diagram 3, then open up the prongs of the paper fastener on the inside of the box.

For the base of the house, cut two pieces of cardboard 5 mm ($\frac{1}{4}$ in.) larger all round than the base of the box. Stick them together, then cover by gluing on slate paper, cutting it a little larger all round, then turning and sticking the edges on the other side of the cardboard. Stick the base under the house, having the back edge even with the back of the house.

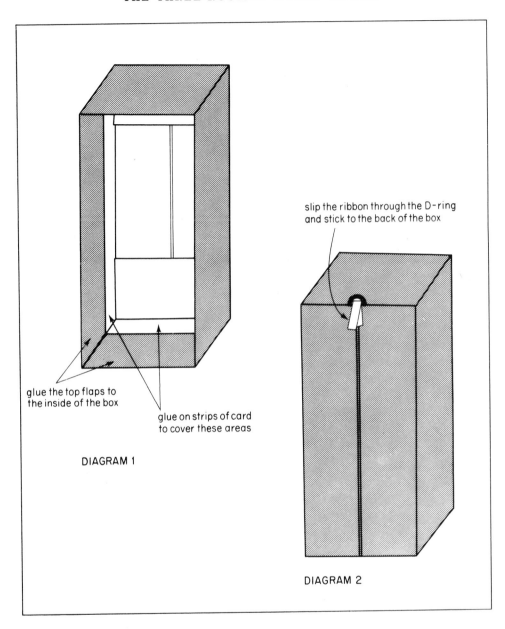

slip the ribbon through the D-ring
and stick to the back of the box

glue the top flaps to
the inside of the box

glue on strips of card
to cover these areas

DIAGRAM 1

DIAGRAM 2

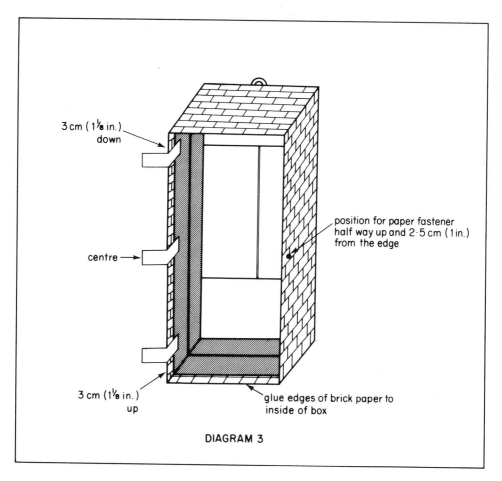

3 cm (1⅛ in.)
down

centre →

position for paper fastener
half way up and 2·5 cm (1 in.)
from the edge

3 cm (1⅛ in.)
up

glue edges of brick paper to
inside of box

DIAGRAM 3

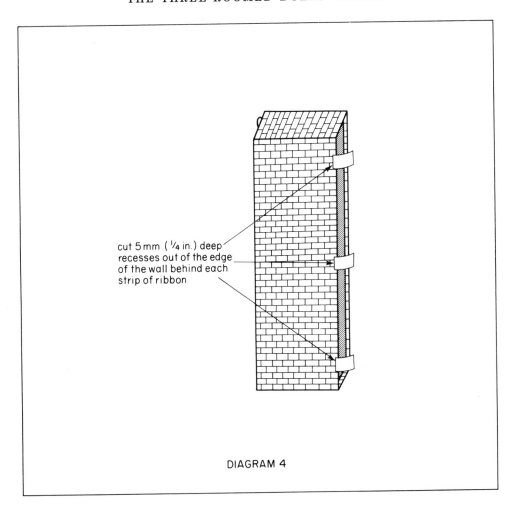

cut 5 mm (¼ in.) deep
recesses out of the edge
of the wall behind each
strip of ribbon

DIAGRAM 4

To make the walls, floors and ceilings inside the house

The walls and floors are pieces of strong card cut to size. Work on one room at a time. The card should be fairly rigid and not easily bent. These pieces of card are covered with fabric or paper before sticking in place inside the house. This method also considerably strengthens the whole structure of the house. In the house illustrated, the walls of the sitting room and the main bedroom are about 14 cm (5½ in.) high. This leaves a slightly smaller space at the top of the house for the nursery.

Begin with the sitting-room on the ground floor. Measure the size of the floor area and cut a piece of card to fit. Cut a piece of fabric or paper a little larger all round than the card, stick it to the card, then turn the edges to the other side and stick them down. All the pieces of card are covered in this way. Stick the sitting-room floor in position inside the house. Next measure the back wall of the sitting room, which will be about 14 cm (5½ in.) in height, then cut a piece of card to fit. Cover the card, then stick the back wall in place inside the house. Measure, cut out and cover the side walls of the sitting-room in the same way.

The sitting-room ceiling, which also forms the bedroom floor will be supported on the top edges of the pieces of card which form the sitting-room walls. Cut the piece of card to fit, then cover it with some fabric or paper which is suitable for the bedroom floor. Next cut a piece of plain paper to fit the other side of the card, and stick it in place to form the sitting-room ceiling below. Stick the floor in place on the top edges of the sitting-room walls.

Now make the bedroom walls as for the sitting-room walls, and then the bedroom ceiling, which also forms the nursery floor. Cover the nursery ceiling by sticking a piece of plain paper to the inside of the house at the top.

Finally, make the nursery walls as for the other walls, cutting the card pieces to fit the remaining wall space.

To make the front of the house

This consists of two pieces of cardboard, an outer and an inner piece. After making each piece, glue them together, while at the same time sandwiching the ribbon hinges and elastic loop fastening between them.

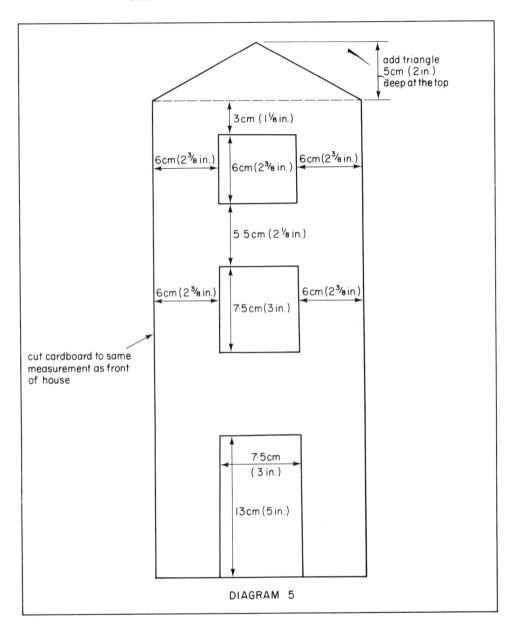

add triangle 5cm (2 in.) deep at the top

3cm (1⅛ in.)

6cm (2⅜ in.)

6cm (2⅜ in.)

6cm (2⅜ in.)

5·5 cm (2⅛ in.)

6cm (2⅜ in.)

6cm (2⅜ in.)

7·5 cm (3 in.)

cut cardboard to same measurement as front of house

7·5 cm (3 in.)

13cm (5 in.)

DIAGRAM 5

Make the outer cardboard piece first. Cut a piece of cardboard to completely cover the front of the house, but also add a triangular shape at the top as shown in diagram 5. Draw on the positions of the windows as shown in diagram 5. These measurements should be adjusted if a box of a different size is used, so that the windows will be placed in the correct positions in relation to the rooms. Cut out the windows using a craft knife held against a ruler.

Now cover the front face of the house with brick paper, cutting it a little larger all round than the cardboard. Turn the edges to the wrong side of the cardboard and stick down. Pierce a hole in the centre of the brick paper covering each window, clip the paper to the corners of the windows then turn it to the wrong side of the cardboard and stick down.

Draw the front door onto the front face of the house, as shown in diagram 5, making it about 7·5 cm by 13 cm (3 in. by 5 in.). Glue on strips of thin card for the door panels, making them about 2 cm ($\frac{3}{4}$ in.) in width. The upper panels are about 6 cm ($2\frac{3}{8}$ in.) long, and the lower panels 4 cm ($1\frac{1}{2}$ in.) long. Paint the door, and also paint about 1 cm ($\frac{3}{8}$ in.) of the brick paper around the edges of the window openings. For the horizontal window struts, cut two 5 mm ($\frac{1}{4}$ in.) wide strips of very thin card, a little longer than the width of the windows. Paint the struts, then lay them aside. When the door is dry, glue on the door knob and knocker.

For the window and door frames cut 1 cm ($\frac{3}{8}$ in.) wide strips of thin card. Glue a strip on either side of the door, then glue a strip across the top of the door, cutting the ends of the strip to an angle as shown in the illustrations. Stick card strips to the sides and tops of the windows leaving about 5 mm ($\frac{1}{4}$ in.) of the painted edges exposed, as shown in the illustrations.

For the window sills glue on strips of card cut a little wider than the window frames and long enough to fit underneath the windows and window frames with a little extra added at each side.

Cut a triangle of thin card to fit above the door frame about 2·5 cm (1 in.) deep, then glue it in place. Cut a triangle of thin card to fit the triangular piece at the top of the front face of the house, then glue it in place. Cut another smaller triangle, and glue it to the first one. If desired, stick on a small piece of card, either circular, or in the shape of a shield, then mark on the name and date of the house.

3

4

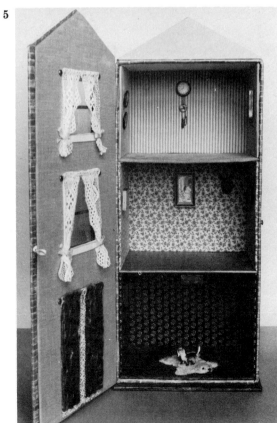

5

On the inside of the windows stick the horizontal window struts, then stick on pieces of acetate film for the window glass cut about 2 cm ($\frac{3}{4}$ in.) larger all round than the windows.

For the inner cardboard piece of the front face of the house, cut a rectangle of cardboard to the same size as the outer piece, then trim off 5 mm ($\frac{1}{4}$ in.) at each long side. Cut out the window openings then cover the cardboard with fabric or paper in the same way as for the outer piece. For the ends of the curtain rods above the windows, fix in a paper fastener a little to the sides of the windows, then open up the prongs of the paper fastener on the wrong side of the cardboard. Fix in paper fasteners, also, to denote the ends of the curtain rod above the door, about 15 cm (6 in.) up from the lower edge and 10 cm (4 in.) apart.

Now assemble the inner and outer cardboard pieces of the front face of the house. Place the inner piece centrally in position over the front of the house, having the fabric-covered side facing in towards the rooms. Glue the remaining free halves of the ribbon hinges onto the back of this piece, and also glue a loop of elastic in position at the opposite edge to line up with the paper fastener on the house wall. Keeping the inner cardboard piece in position, spread it liberally with glue, especially over the ribbon and elastic, then place the wrong side of the outer cardboard piece onto it. Press both pieces firmly together until the glue is dry.

Cut 1 cm ($\frac{3}{8}$ in.) wide strips of thin card and stick under each window on the inner piece, for the window sills. Also stick very narrow strips along the lower edges of the windows to meet the card window sills and the acetate film. Cut bits of lace trimming or edging for curtains and stick them in place as shown in the illustrations. Stick on a bit of fabric trimmed with narrow lace edging for the door curtain, gluing it into folds.

Now make the apex roof on the house itself. Close the front face of the house then measure the sides of the top triangular piece. Cut a piece of card to this length, making it wide enough to cover the top of the house from front to back. Bend the card across the centre to make the apex shape then glue on slate paper, cutting it a little larger all round, and gluing the surplus onto the wrong side. Stick the side edges of the roof to the top of the house at each side. Now cut triangles of card to fit the gaps at the front and back of the apex roof, and stick them in place.

Materials Required for Furnishings

The materials required are mentioned in the instructions for each item. However, a few helpful suggestions are given here.

Household packaging

The secret of getting together suitable material for furnishing the house is to always be on the look out for anything at all which might be of use. All types of household and food packaging should be scrutinized before discarding to see if there are any small boxes, lids, caps etc. which could be saved. Small boxes made of thin card are particularly good for making items of furniture, and larger boxes will provide a supply of thin card for cutting up.

Colouring

Enamel paints, sold in small tins for colouring plastic model soldiers etc. can be obtained in a good colour range. However, to quickly colour small items made of plastic or card, felt-tipped permanent marker pens can be used instead. Black and brown are the most useful colours.

Chapter Two

Glue

A quick-drying all-purpose adhesive (such as UHU) should be used for sticking all the different types of materials. Unwanted smears of this adhesive can be removed by dabbing with a little acetone or methylated spirit.

Tweezers

A pair of tweezers, if available, will prove to be extremely helpful when positioning and sticking small objects together.

Compasses

Use a pair of compasses when drawing out the circular patterns mentioned in the instructions.

CHAPTER THREE

Interior Decoration

Plaster ceilings and mouldings

Cover the walls with fabric or paper in the usual way then stick strips of white paper along the upper parts of the walls to cover about a quarter of the way down. The ceiling should also be covered with white paper. For the fancy plaster mouldings use the embossed paper strips which can be found on birthday and Christmas cake paper frills. These are usually gold or silver on one side and plain white on the other side. Stick strips round the edges of the ceiling and tops of the walls having the white side of the strip outside. If desired, a raised strip can be stuck on where the ceiling and walls meet. Fold the embossed paper strip to form a triangular shape and stick it in place as shown in illustration 6. For a circular moulding at the centre of the roof where the ceiling rose is fixed, use the centre from an embossed paper doyley as shown in the illustration.

Picture rails

A picture rail is required to cover the join where the plaster meets the wallpaper. Cut a narrow strip of thin card the length of the wall, then

another, narrower than the first. Stick the narrowest strip to the first strip, having it even with one edge which will be the top edge. Colour the rail, then stick in place on the wall.

Skirting boards

Cut strips of card about 2·5 cm (1 in.) in width. Colour them then stick in place all round the lower edges of the walls.

Floor coverings and wallpaper

Illustration 7 shows a selection of printed and woven fabrics suitable for use as wall and floor coverings. For bare floor boards, cover the floor with brown wrapping paper then mark on boards and nails with pencil.

(above) The master bedroom

2

(below) The living room

3　The three-storey dolls' house (open)

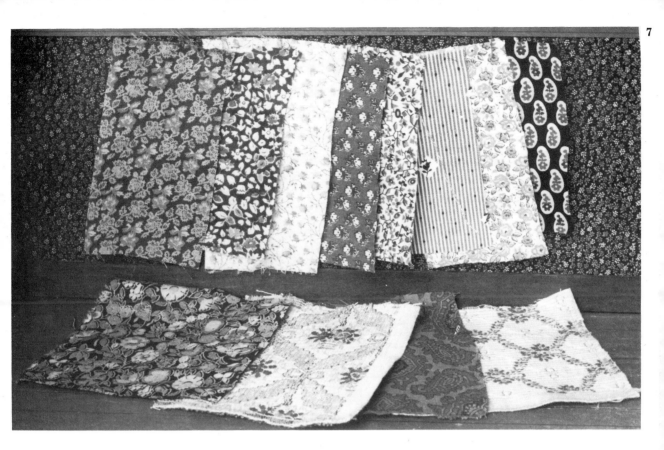

Doors

Make false doors on the inside walls of the house from thin card in the same way as for the outside door of the three-roomed dolls' house.

Windows

If desired, false windows can be made on the inside walls. Stick a picture postcard with a suitable photographic view to the wall. Make the frame, curtains and windowsills in the same way as for the three-roomed house.

CHAPTER FOUR

The Staircase

In the Victorian-style dolls' house the staircase may be a false one rising up to ceiling height but without an opening in the floor above. A portion of the next floor can of course be cut away if desired to make a proper staircase. An enclosed stair between two walls is very easy to make from several

small boxes. Matchboxes and thin card cigar boxes are ideal. Illustration 8 shows how to construct the staircase by gluing the boxes together with each box making one step. The back ends of the boxes, forming the top steps, may have to be cut shorter to make them even with the lower steps, as shown in the illustration. Illustration 9 shows the staircase painted and in position against one wall of the house, ready for the wall at the other side of the stairs to be glued in place. For stair carpet use ribbon, either plain or patterned, and glue it in place.

The Fireplace & Accessories

The central part of the fireplace shown in illustration 10 is made from part of a card gift box, but the tray of a matchbox or other similar box can be used. First cut a piece of card to fit on top of the box tray then cut out an arched shape about 5 cm (2 in.) high to form the fireplace opening. Stick the card to the box tray. For the front of the grate cut a strip of card about 1·5 cm ($\frac{5}{8}$ in.) wide and a little longer than the width of the fireplace opening so that it will form a curved shape when in position. Stick the short edges of the card to each side of the fireplace opening, then fix a paper fastener in the centre for a knob. Stick two narrow strips of card above this for the bars of the grate, curving them in the same way. Now stick a strip of narrow braid around the fireplace opening for an ornamental effect. Paint the entire fireplace black.

For the mantel supports on either side of the fireplace cut two pieces of card about 6 cm (2$\frac{3}{8}$ in.) wide by the height of the fireplace. Fold the cards equally three times along the length, forming two square columns, then stick the long edges together. Paint the columns to resemble wood or white marble mottled with black. Stick the columns in place on either side of the

fireplace. For the mantel piece cut a piece of card to fit over the fireplace adding a little extra to jut out at the front and sides. Paint to match the columns and then stick a bit of ribbon or braid round the edge of the mantelpiece for a valance as shown in illustration 10. Stick the mantelpiece in place.

For the tiled hearth use a strip of card painted or covered with paper and ruled into squares with a pencil.

For the coal fire glue bits of black, red and yellow paper into the grate. For the flames use scraps of red cellophane and wisps of cotton wool for smoke.

Fender

A most attractive brass fender can be made from a strip of gold braid. The braid used on the fender in illustration 11 is 2·5 cm (1 in.) wide. Cut a piece

of braid to the required length then fold one long edge of the braid over a pipe cleaner and glue in place. Bend the fender into shape.

Poker and stand

The black cat poker stand shown in the illustration is a lucky charm. Make the poker from a cocktail stick cut to 4 cm ($1\frac{1}{2}$ in.) in length, then stick a bead to the blunt end of the poker for the handle.

CHAPTER SIX

Wall Ornaments

Pictures and frames

Tiny reproductions of pictures are often found in magazines advertising for sale prints of famous paintings. These can be framed in a variety of ways. Picture frames for dolls' houses can be bought and when painted gold or brown these are quite suitable for the Victorian house.

Miniature gold photograph frames can be purchased at reasonable prices. These are usually very ornamental and when used for framing suitable small pictures they make splendid 'large' paintings for the miniature house. A frame of this type is shown in the centre of illustration 12.

Small belt buckles of all types can be used by removing the centre prongs and then sticking the pictures in place on the centre bars. Large flat buttons with pictures glued in the centre are also very effective for circular framed pictures.

A few items of jewellery can also be used as shown in illustration 12. A brooch framing a piece of needlework makes a tapestry picture and a cameo ear-ring and small mosaic brooch are also shown.

Mirrors

Small mirror tiles, handbag mirrors or circular mirrors for hanging in bird cages are all useful. Frame these by sticking gold or brown braid round the edges.

Clocks

Tiny clock faces can be cut out of magazines. They may be found in advertisements for wrist watches or photographs showing rooms with clocks in them.

The wall clock shown in illustration 12 is made from a small gilt buckle with a piece of an ear-ring fitting for the pendulum. The weights are pieces from a slide-in type of necklace clasp and they are suspended from threads glued to the back of the clock.

Trophies

For the stag's head trophy shown in the illustration cut the head off a plastic toy stag then mount this by gluing it into an oval piece of card.

For the fishing trophy cut a 1 cm ($\frac{3}{8}$ in.) section off one end of the slide-on cover of a matchbox. Stick a piece of acetate film to one side for the glass then cut a piece of blue card to fit the other side. Make a fish from Plasticine to fit on the card and glue it in place with bits of green foam sponge for the weeds. Glue the card in place, then stick a bit of braid or ribbon round the edge of the matchbox section for the frame.

Ornaments

Paperweights and small dishes

Most households have a button box which contains a mixture of buttons accumulated over a number of years, and which should yield a few treasures suitable for the dolls' house. Illustration 13 shows an assortment of glass, metal, plastic, bone and pearl buttons, and also a tiny fabric button with a Union Jack design. Tiny pictures can be stuck underneath glass buttons to make them resemble glass paperweights.

Glass domes

The large capsule shown in illustration 14 comes from a bubble-gum vending machine. These machines can usually be found located outside sweet shops and the capsules which they dispense contain lucky charms or tiny plastic toys. These can also be of use in the dolls' house. Similarly shaped clear plastic domed lids can sometimes be found on eye make-up and other cosmetic containers.

To make the base on the largest dome, cut a circle of card to fit, then press

on a small lump of Plasticine. Push dried flowers and grasses into the Plasticine, then stick the base in place under the dome. Stick a strip of black paper round the lower edge of the dome.

The smaller domes shown in the illustration are halves of gelatine capsules normally used for medicinal purposes. A friendly chemist will probably be able to supply a few empty ones in various sizes. For the bases on these domes use plain black trouser buttons turned upside down. For the very tiny dome shown in the illustration a small flat bead is used.

Sea shells
Use small shells, as shown in illustration 15, for specimen sea shells displayed around the house.

Potted plants, vases and flower containers

The oriental slipper and boot flower containers shown in illustration 15 are inexpensive lucky charms, painted white to resemble china. The elegant tall black vase filled with grasses and flowers is simply a push-on cap off a felt-tipped marker pen. A tiny perfume bottle is also shown in the illustration.

For the large potted plant pots, screw-on plastic lids are used of the type shown in the illustration. They are about 2·5 cm (1 in.) in diameter and 2 cm ($\frac{3}{4}$ in.) deep. Make the lids more decorative by painting or sticking bits of fancy braid around them. For the soil inside the pots press in lumps of Plasticine. Cut the pointed leaf shapes from green paper, then push them into the Plasticine. Cut the leaves for the tall plant from a fan-shaped piece of paper, then glue them to stems cut off dried flowers. Fix the stems into the Plasticine.

Candles and oil lamps

The base of the oil lamp in illustration 16 is made from a toggle off an anorak draw-string plus two beads for the remainder. A match-stick, pared down slightly, holds them all together. Glue the beads and toggle onto the match-stick as shown in the illustration, then for the glass chimney at the top, glue in a bit cut off the end of a plastic ball-point pen refill tube.

The tiny glass candle stick is a button with a birthday cake candle glued on.

For the other candle holder shown in illustration 16 a small plastic lid painted gold is used, with a piece of wire fixed on for a handle. The candle here is a section of pared down match-stick with a bit of black thread for the wick.

Mantel clock

Cut a small section off one end of a match-box tray for the clock and paint it black. Stick on a clock face cut from a magazine, then glue a piece of card under the base and a strip of thin braid round the top. A fancy button painted black is glued to the top of the clock shown in illustration 16.

Animals and figures

The gold sea-creatures in illustration 17 are in reality miniature ornaments, and these make a pair of very grand mantelpiece decorations in the dolls' house.

The elephant is a lucky charm. The statue of the child is a plastic cake decoration used on christening or birthday cakes. It is painted white, and glued onto a button for the base.

Framed photographs

Illustration 17 shows two double heart-shaped frames. One is an old locket with a bit of wire fixed around the centre to make it stand up. The other is a brown plastic hair slide, with the wire grip at the back bent to form the support.

The circular frame is a scrap of jewellery with a piece of bent card glued to the back for a stand.

8

Books
The book shown in illustration 17 is simply a piece of thin card, folded, then coloured black. For book titles, search through magazines and any other printed matter to find suitable words in the tiniest possible print.

Oddments
Illustration 18 shows a selection of odds and ends which can be used for ornaments. There are beads, ear-rings, a brooch and other bits of jewellery.

Christmas tree
The type of tree used for decorating Christmas cakes is shown in illustration 18. Trim the tree by sticking tiny beads among the branches and winding round thin gold or silver thread for tinsel. The star at the top of the tree is an ear-ring.

Hard Furniture

Purchased dolls' house items

Although a selection of Victorian-style furniture can be obtained from toy shops, these are usually made in colours which are unsuitable for the Victorian home. The plastic furniture shown in illustration 19 has all been re-painted with dark brown enamel paint.

For the upholstery on the dining room chairs, pieces of velvet are cut to fit and glued in place.

Tables

Rectangular, square and round tables can be made very easily from lids or boxes if floor-level tablecloths are glued over them so that the items beneath are completely hidden. Illustration 20 shows a selection of suitable boxes and plastic lids, and also one round and rectangular table covered with fabric.

To cover the table with fabric, place the bit of fabric for the tablecloth over the lid or box, then mark all round where the fabric touches ground level. Cut the fabric as marked, then neaten the raw edges by gluing on lace

trimming. Stick the cloth to the top of the table, and also stick it to the sides of the box or lid so that it hangs down in natural folds as shown in the illustration.

Bamboo tables and pedestals

The items in illustration 21 are all made from different sizes of plastic hair rollers, as shown in the illustration. First of all, if the roller has spikes, cut these off using a craft knife. Next, decide on the required height of the table, then cut one end off the roller shortening it to this measurement. The largest diameter table shown in the illustration is made from a jumbo size roller and it is 5 cm (2 in.) in height. To get the lumpy bamboo effect use scissors to roughly snip away strips of plastic between the sections. Begin at the lower end of the table and snip the sections away to leave four legs then snip sections away above the legs as shown in the illustration. Paint the table a natural bamboo shade. For the table top cut a circle of card to fit, cover it with natural coloured fabric and stick in position.

Plant stands and pedestals

The marble column pedestal shown in illustration 22 is made from two plastic pill-bottle lids and the slide-on cover off a tube of lipstick. The pedestal is painted white. Two cotton reels painted brown are also shown in the illustration.

Whatnot

For the legs of the whatnot shown in illustration 23 four cocktail sticks, four oval beads and four round beads are required. The shelves are rectangles of card edged with strips cut off the gold paper braid on a birthday cake frill. To keep the shelves at the correct height on the legs, use small cuttings off the empty end of a plastic ball-point pen refill tube.

For each shelf cut a 5·5 cm by 3 cm ($2\frac{1}{8}$ in. by $1\frac{1}{8}$ in.) piece of card. Carefully make a small hole close to the corner of each piece of card just large enough for the cocktail stick legs to be pushed through. Glue one end of each leg into an oval bead. Push a section of the plastic tube onto each leg about 1 cm ($\frac{3}{8}$ in.) above the bead. Now slip the first shelf in position, pushing a leg through each corner, and spreading the top of each section of plastic tube with glue. Position the next shelf then the top shelf in the same way, spacing them at 2 cm ($\frac{3}{4}$ in.) intervals. Now cut off the tops of the cocktail sticks if necessary, leaving just enough to glue inside the round beads.

Cut thin strips off the paper braid, and glue round the edge of each shelf. Put the whatnot aside until the glue is completely dry, making sure that the legs are quite parallel to each other. The whatnot should be quite stable when the glue is dry, and it can then be painted.

Screens

The four-wing screen in illustration 24 is simply a piece of card folded concertina-wise, and covered with fabric. Cut a 10 cm by 12 cm (4 in. by 4¾ in.) piece of card and fold it three times at even intervals along the length. Stick on a piece of fabric, turning and gluing the raw edges to the wrong side of the screen. Cover the wrong side with paper.

The two-wing screen in illustration 24 is made by sticking bits of children's paper scraps onto pieces of card. Cut two rectangles of card measuring about 4·5 cm by 11·5 cm (1¾ in. by 4½ in.). Stick a small picture scrap in the centre of each one, then cut tiny motifs off other scraps and stick them all round the centre pictures until the cards are completely covered. The illustration also shows a selection of scraps in front of the screens printed with suitable small designs.

To frame the edges of the screen, cut very narrow strips of thin card, colour them black, then stick them around the edges of each wing. To make the hinge joining the two wings together, stick a strip of paper to the back between the two wings, leaving a space between the edges so that the screen can be folded.

Washstand

Begin with a small box for the drawer, or a cutting from a box measuring about 1·5 cm by 3 cm by 6 cm ($\frac{5}{8}$ in. by $1\frac{1}{8}$ in. by $2\frac{3}{8}$ in.). Paint the box then fix two paper fasteners in the front for the drawer knobs, as shown in illustration 25. Next make the marble top by cutting a piece of card a little larger all round than the drawer but keeping it flush with the back edge. Cover the top with white paper then paint to resemble marble. Cut the side legs of the washstand from fairly thick card using the pattern shown in diagram 6. Stick one to each side of the drawer then cut a 2 cm ($\frac{3}{4}$ in.) wide strip of card for the lower shelf to fit between the legs. Cut thin strips of

51

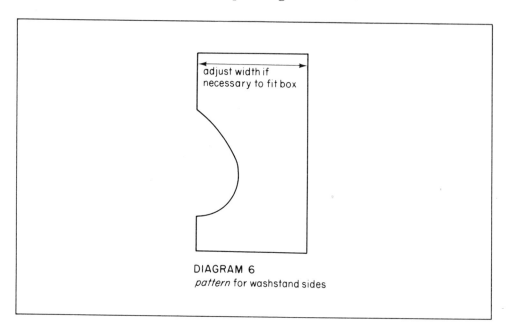

DIAGRAM 6
pattern for washstand sides

card for shelf supports and stick these under the shelf at each side when gluing the shelf in position. Paint the legs and shelf. Cut a rectangle of card for the back of the washstand measuring about 5 cm by 6·5 cm (2 in. by $2\frac{1}{2}$ in.). Cut the top edge to a curved shape then cut out a rectangle at the centre, leaving a frame as shown in the illustration. Stick on bits of paper doyley to resemble carved decoration, then paint the frame. Cut a piece of card a little larger than the inner edge of the frame, cover with paper and paint to match the marble top of the washstand. Stick the piece of card to the back of the frame, then stick the back of the washstand in position. Cut a thin strip of card for the towel rail, bend round the ends, and stick them to one side of the stand as shown in the illustration.

The bowl and jug shown on the washstand are taken from a dolls' china tea set. The hair brush is a dolls' plastic one. The soap dish is a small button with a tiny piece of soap glued on.

For the towel, cut a small strip of fabric and fray out the edges.

(above) The nursery   5   (below) The kitchen

6   (above) The milliner's shop

7   (left) The dolls' house (closed)

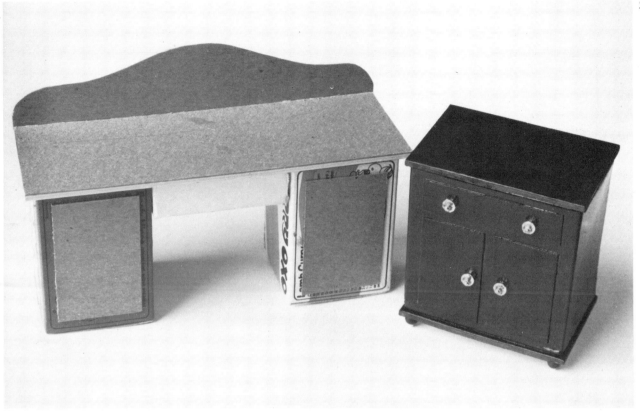

Drawers and cupboards

False drawers and cupboards are very easy to make from small boxes. For the best results the boxes should be in good condition and not bent or dented. Illustration 26 shows a two-door cupboard with a drawer at the top, made from half of a box which had contained a large tube of glue. It measures 6·5 cm by 4 cm by 6·5 cm ($2\frac{1}{2}$ in. by $1\frac{1}{2}$ in. by $2\frac{1}{2}$ in.). Pieces of card, cut a little larger, are glued to the top and base of the box, then pieces of thin card are glued in place for the drawer and cupboard doors. For all the knobs use small glass beads spread with a little glue and fixed into the card with pins. Make legs on the cupboard in the same way as the knobs.

The illustration also shows three boxes assembled to make a sideboard. Desks, wardrobes, chests of drawers and dressing tables can all be made in the same way. For carved ornamentation stick on pieces of embossed paper cut off doyleys before painting.

27

adjust height and
width if necessary

DIAGRAM 7
pattern for coal box sides

Kitchen dresser

Illustration 27 shows how a kitchen dresser can be made by simply adding an upper portion with shelves to the cupboard already described. Thick card is used for the sides, top and shelves. For the cup hooks, push short pins into the edge of the card shelf.

Coal box

This is made from a section cut off one end of a small oblong box which had contained lolly sticks. Similar boxes can be found on tubes of glue, toothpaste etc. The finished coal box is about 3·5 cm ($1\frac{3}{8}$ in.) square at the base and 2·5 cm (1 in.) high.

Cut a 2·5 cm (1 in.) piece off one end of the box leaving on the tuck-in flap as shown in illustration 28. Stick a piece of card to the cut end to close it in completely. Cut the side pieces of the box using the pattern shown in diagram 7 adjusting the height and width of the pattern if necessary to suit the size of the box being used. Stick the side pieces in place, then glue the long end flap to the sloping edges of the side pieces. Stick a piece of card underneath the coal box for the base. Paint the box black.

For the handle, a screw-in type of necklace clasp is fixed in place with two glass-headed pins and two beads. These are shown in the illustration. For the hinges use either bits of jewellery or pieces cut off a gold doyley. Decorate the sloping front of the coal box by sticking on strips of gold embossed paper with a flower motif at the centre as shown in the illustration.

28

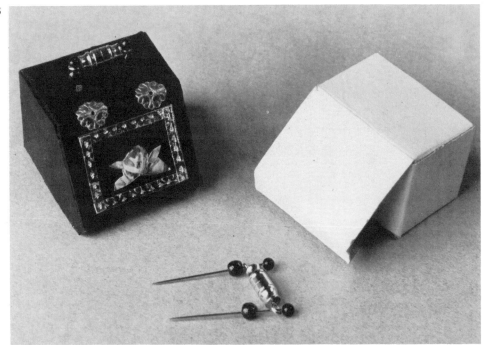

Upholstered Furniture, Cushions and Rugs

Bear skin rug

Make this from short-pile fur fabric. Cut out the rug using the pattern shown in diagram 8.

Cut a piece of red felt to fit underneath the head as shown by the dotted line on the pattern. Stick the felt in place leaving the mouth end open. Push a little cotton wool, for stuffing, inside the head. Stick on two small black beads for the eyes and a tiny bit of black felt for the nose as shown in illustration 29.

Footstools

Round or rectangular stools can be made from small plastic lids and matchbox trays. For the round footstool shown in illustration 29 the lid measures 3 cm ($1\frac{1}{8}$ in.) diameter by 1 cm ($\frac{3}{8}$ in.) deep. Pack the lid with cotton wool as shown, then spread glue all round the side of the lid at the top edge. Cut a piece of fabric a little larger than the diameter of the lid, place it over the cotton wool then press the raw edges onto the glued portion of the lid at the same time as stretching it over the cotton wool.

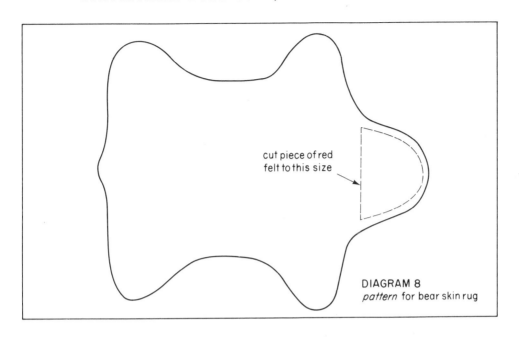

cut piece of red
felt to this size

DIAGRAM 8
pattern for bear skin rug

Glue round a bit of braid to hide the raw edges of the fabric. For the rectangular stool cut the matchbox tray in half then slide and glue one half inside the other as shown in the illustration. Stuff the box and cover with fabric and braid as for the round footstool. Make small feet under the footstool by pushing a pin through a small bead at each corner.

Half-tester bed
The mattress part of the bed shown in illustration 30 is about 7·5 cm (3 in.) wide by 11 cm (4¼ in.) long by 2·5 cm (1 in.) deep. If a suitable lid of this size is not available then the bed can be constructed as shown in the illustration. Here a small lid of the correct width is cut in half, then a half is glued to each end of a 7·5 cm by 11 cm (3 in. by 4¼ in.) piece of card for the top of the mattress. Cover the card mattress with a piece of fabric cut a little larger all round, placing a layer of cotton wool between the card and the fabric. Stick the raw edges of the fabric onto the sides and ends of the mattress. Glue a strip of 2·5 cm (1 in.) wide ribbon all round the sides and ends of the mattress to cover the raw edges of the fabric and also the card.

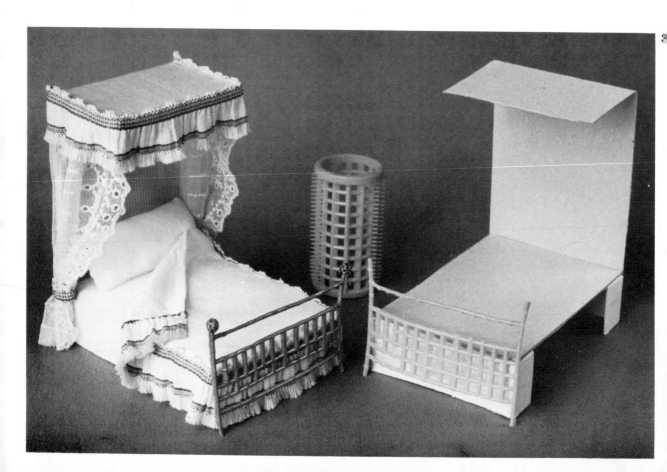

To make the bed head, cut a 7·5 cm by 18 cm (3 in. by 7 in.) piece of card. Fold over 5 cm (2 in.) at one end for the canopy. Cover the bed head by sticking on a piece of fabric then stick it in position as shown in the illustration. Use strips of lace edging or fabric to make curtains, gluing the top edges to each side of the canopy, then gather the curtains to each side of the bed with a strip of ribbon or braid as shown in the illustration. Now glue fancy braid or a length of gathered ribbon all round the edge of the canopy.

For the bolster pillow cut two 4 cm by 9 cm (1$\frac{1}{2}$ in. by 3$\frac{1}{2}$ in.) strips of fabric. Sew them together all round the edges, taking a narrow seam, and leaving a gap for turning. Turn and stuff the pillow with cotton wool, then slip stitch the gap.

For the bed-spread cut a piece of fabric a little larger all round than the top of the bed, then stick braid or ribbon to match the canopy all round the edges except for the pillow edge. Turn in the pillow edge and stick down to neaten.

To make the brass bed end, a plastic hair roller is required. Cut the ends off the roller, then cut it open along the length. If the roller has spikes cut them off using a craft knife. To flatten the roller, press it, using a warm iron over a damp cloth, then, while the plastic is still warm, place it under a heavy object such as a book.

Cut the roller to the required height and width of the bed end. Now use scissors or a craft knife to carefully cut away sections of the plastic, trimming away the pieces as neatly as possible to leave smooth strips of plastic. The illustration shows a hair roller and also a bed end in preparation with some of the sections already cut away.

Paint the bed end with gold paint and stick on beads for knobs.
Glue the bed end to the foot of the bed.

Upholstered chair

The chair shown in illustration 31 is extremely easy to make using a plastic lid for the seat. A fringe glued around the seat of the chair hides the lid beneath. The lid illustrated is 4·5 cm (1$\frac{3}{4}$ in.) in diameter and 2·5 cm (1 in.) deep.

First of all pack the lid firmly with cotton wool as shown. Cut a circle of fabric about 1 cm ($\frac{3}{8}$ in.) larger all round than the diameter of the lid. Spread glue all round the side of the lid at the top edge then place the fabric circle over the cotton wool. Press the raw edges onto the glued portion all round, while at the same time stretching the fabric over the cotton wool.

Now cut the chair back from thin card using the solid line shown on the pattern in diagram 9. This pattern can be made smaller or larger if necessary to suit a smaller or larger lid. Cut a piece of fabric to the size of the dotted line shown in diagram 9. Place the card in position on the wrong side of the fabric then clip the curved edges of the fabric all round. Turn the clipped edges over and stick them to the card but do not turn over and stick the lower edge. Now stuff cotton wool between the fabric and the card to pad the back of the chair. Turn in the lower raw edge of the fabric and stick it onto the card as for the other edges.

To make the buttoned effect on the chair back make rows of tiny stitches, taking the thread through from the back of the card into the fabric, and pulling the thread up tight. Work the rows of stitches as shown on the chair back pattern. To cover the raw edges of the fabric at the back, cut a piece of

3

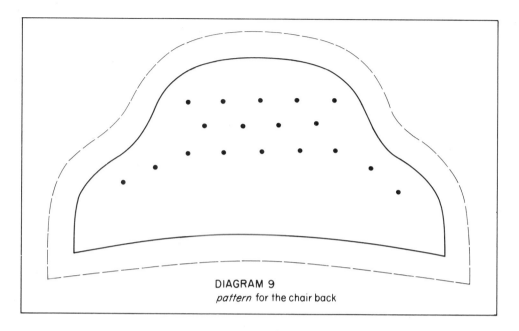

DIAGRAM 9
pattern for the chair back

fabric a little larger all round than the solid line on the pattern. Turn in and stick down all the raw edges to neaten, then stick this piece to the chair back.

Stick 1 cm ($\frac{3}{8}$ in.) at the lower edge of the chair back onto the seat, using pins stuck into the fabric to hold it in position until the glue dries. Now glue a fringe round the chair to conceal the plastic lid. The fringe on the chair shown in the illustration is a strip cut off the selvedge of the fabric and frayed out.

Chairs with rectangular seats can be made in the same way, using small boxes for the seats, or an oblong box can be used to make a chaise longue or sofa.

Upholstered sofa with legs

For the sofa seat in illustration 32 a card cigar box measuring 5·5 cm by 11 cm by 1 cm ($2\frac{1}{8}$ in. by $4\frac{1}{4}$ in. by $\frac{3}{8}$ in.) is used.

Pad the top of the seat with a layer of cotton wool, then cover with a piece of fabric cut large enough to turn and stick the raw edges underneath the box. For the back and sides of the sofa, cut a 4 cm ($1\frac{1}{2}$ in.) wide strip of thin card long enough to go across the back and along each side of the sofa. Round off the corners at the front top edges of the card. Now cover the card with fabric, pad out and make buttoned stitching in the same way as for the back of the upholstered chair.

For the sofa legs, use beads threaded onto pins, pushing a pin in each corner of the sofa underneath.

Cushions and rugs

Use strips of braid or fancy ribbon. Cut squares or rectangles for cushions and stitch them together all round the edges, pushing in a bit of cotton wool for stuffing. Stick lace edging or other trimmings round the edges, as shown on the cushions in illustration 32.

Rugs can also be made from strips of braid or ribbon, with the ends frayed out to make a fringe.

The Nursery

Child's bed

The bed in illustration 33 is 7 cm (2¾ in.) long, 4 cm (1½ in.) wide and 2 cm (¾ in.) deep. The mattress is made from a box, and the ends from a plastic hair roller, in exactly the same way as given for the half-tester bed.

Rocking horse

Use a plastic toy pony for this. The one in the illustration is 4·5 cm ($1\frac{3}{4}$ in.) in height. Paint the pony with dappled spots, then, when the paint is dry, press the front and back legs outwards splaying them apart.

For the rockers, stick together three layers of thin card, bending the card into a shallow curved shape before the glue dries. From the curved card, cut two rockers measuring about 3 mm ($\frac{1}{8}$ in.) in width by 6·5 cm ($2\frac{1}{2}$ in.) long. Glue the pony's feet to the rockers then stick a card strut across the rockers between the pony's front and back legs as shown in the illustration. Paint the rockers.

For the saddle, stick a small piece of felt across the pony's back, and glue on threads for reins as shown in the illustration.

Blackboard and easel

Cut a 3 cm by 4 cm ($1\frac{1}{8}$ in. by $1\frac{1}{2}$ in.) piece of card for the board and paint it black. For the easel cut strips of card and stick them together as shown in diagram 10. Stick the board to the easel.

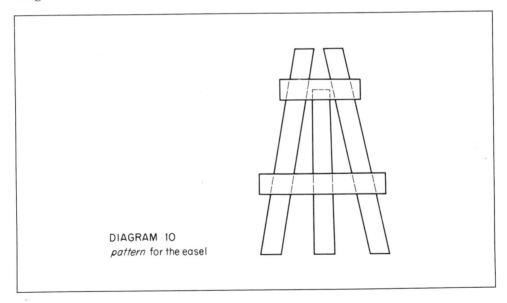

DIAGRAM 10
pattern for the easel

Doll

Use a small bead for the doll's head and paint on the hair and face. Stick a short length of pipe cleaner into the head for the body and around this glue a piece of fabric for the dress.

Toys

Several items suitable for dolls' house toys are shown in illustration 33. The duck is a plastic farmyard toy. The trumpet, rabbit and elephant on wheels are lucky charms. A card base is stuck underneath the elephant, and the wheels are sections cut off an empty plastic ball-point pen refill tube. The wooden train is a miniature ornament.

CHAPTER ELEVEN

Table-ware, Cutlery Etc.

An excellent selection of tiny dolls' house table-ware and cutlery can be obtained from most good toy shops, and some of these are shown in illustration 34. The plates, cups and pans can be painted over in more suitable colours or patterns as shown, using enamel paints.

The tiny glass jars on the kitchen dresser in the illustration are taken from novelty jewellery pendants.

34

Food

Illustration 35 shows a selection of dolls' house food which can be made from a self-hardening type of modelling clay such as DAS. Care should be taken to keep the modelled items to scale, and a few suggestions follow with the sizes given for each item. After modelling, leave to harden, then colour with enamel paints. Metal lids off small tins make excellent pie tins, and other plastic lids can be used for large serving plates.

Bowl of fruit
Make the apples and oranges the size of small peas. Join a few tapered sausage shapes together for bananas and bend into a curve. Roll small balls for the pears a little larger than the apples, then form into shape. Roll very tiny balls for the grapes and join them together. For the pineapple, roll a ball about 1·5 cm ($\frac{5}{8}$ in.) in diameter, and form into an oval shape. Make the impressions all round the pineapple with the slightly parted points of small scissors. Add a few small spear-shaped bits of clay at the top of the pineapple.

Roast chicken or turkey

Begin with a 2 cm ($\frac{3}{4}$ in.) diameter ball of clay for the body. Form it into shape making a ridge for the sharp breast bone at the top. Roll two pea-sized balls for the legs, form into shape, and stick in place, then stick on two small sausage shapes for the wings.

Rolled roast beef, potatoes and carrots

Begin with a 2 cm ($\frac{3}{4}$ in.) diameter ball of clay, then form into shape as shown in the illustration. Make the impressions of the string tied around the beef with a length of thread. Roll uneven shaped balls about the size of small peas for potatoes and carrots. Make the eyes on the potatoes with the point of a needle and roll the carrots against a flat surface to taper them. For the parsley garnish use bits cut off a loofah and paint them green.

Loaves
The illustration shows loaves measuring about 1 cm by 1 cm by 1·5 cm ($\frac{3}{8}$ in. by $\frac{3}{8}$ in. by $\frac{5}{8}$ in.) with two slices cut off one loaf. This can be done with a craft knife while the clay is still moist.

Cherry cake
Begin with a 2 cm ($\frac{3}{4}$ in.) diameter ball. Form into shape and paint on the cherries when completing the cake.

Pie
Fill a small flat lid with clay, then make the impressions all round the edge of the pie with the eye of a needle. Snip the centre of the pie with the points of the scissors.

Plum pudding
Roll a 2 cm ($\frac{3}{4}$ in.) diameter ball, then gently dot the pudding all over with a pencil point. Cut tiny holly leaves from green paper and stick to the top of the pudding.

Further suggestions
Also shown in the illustration are a pan containing egg, bacon and sausages, a wedge of cheese, a plate of crumpets, and a bowl of white and brown eggs.

Household Pets

Chapter Thirteen

Dogs

The dogs shown in illustration 36 are inexpensive plastic ornaments of the type which can usually be purchased from gift or souvenir shops. The dogs' bowls are small lids off tubes of sweets and the bones are made from modelling clay.

Goldfish in a tank

The tank is made from a section cut off a clear flexible plastic tube which had contained tacks, as shown in illustration 36. A strip of acetate film can be used as an alternative, joining the ends of the strip to make the required tank shape. The tank measures about 3 cm ($1\frac{1}{8}$ in.)) by 1·5 cm ($\frac{5}{8}$ in.) by 2 cm ($\frac{3}{4}$ in.) deep. Gently bend the plastic to form a rectangular shape, then cut a piece of card to fit inside the lower edge for the base. Stick the base in place, then press in a little Plasticine for sand and add a few lumps for rocks.

Use bits of loofah painted green for the weeds, then cut small fish from orange paper and glue them to the weeds and rocks. Finally stick a narrow strip of black paper round the outside of the base.

The Peg Dolls

Mother, father and baby are all easy to make from the old-fashioned type of wooden clothes peg shown in illustration 37. The arms are flexible, since they are made from pipe cleaners, and they can be bent into various positions. The mother doll can also be posed sitting down because the legs of the peg are cut away altogether for female dolls. However her stiff skirt will also support her in a standing position. Male dolls made from pegs cannot of course be placed in a seated position, but chapter 15 describes how to make a fully flexible doll for male figures.

Mother
Cut the legs off the peg as shown by the line marked A in the illustration. Mark the face on the head then glue a few strands of sewing thread at the front for the hair. Cover the remainder of the head by sticking on a scrap of lace trimming for a cap. For the blouse, cover the peg from the neck downwards by sticking round a strip of fabric.

For the arms cut a 14 cm (5½ in.) length of pipe cleaner. Bend round 1 cm (⅜ in.) at each end of the cleaner for the hands. To cover each hand, cut a small circle about 1·5 cm (⅝ in.) diameter off an old nylon stocking or pair of nylon tights. Put each hand in the centre of a circle, then pull and gather up the raw edges along the arms. Stick the raw edges of the fabric in this position. For the blouse sleeves cut a 4 cm by 10 cm (1½ in. by 4 in.) strip of fabric. Lap one long edge a little over the other and glue, forming a tube. Push the pipe cleaner arms inside the tube, having the hands protruding at each end of the tube. Now gather up and stick the raw edges of the sleeves around the wrists. Cut very narrow strips of lace edging and stick them

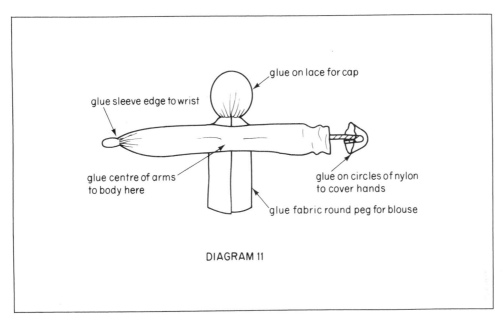

glue on lace for cap

glue sleeve edge to wrist

glue centre of arms
to body here

glue on circles of nylon
to cover hands

glue fabric round peg for blouse

DIAGRAM 11

around the wrists and the neck edge of the blouse. Now stick the centre of the arms in position at the back of the doll just below the neck as shown in diagram 11.

For the skirt, cut a 16 cm (6¼ in.) square of fabric. Fold the square in half and press, noting that the folded edge is now the hem edge of the skirt. Overlap the short edges of the skirt a little and stick them. Turn in the remaining raw edges a little and run round a gathering thread. Put the skirt on the doll, and pull up the gathers round the doll's waist about 1 cm away from the cut lower edge of the peg. Fasten off the thread, and stick the skirt in this position.

For the lacy shoulder pieces on the blouse, use narrow lace edging, sticking it round the back of the neck, over each shoulder, and ending in a V-point at the front just lapping the top edge of the skirt.

Work basket and embroidery   Mother's work basket shown in the illustration is a shallow plastic lid with a strip of braid glued round the side. It contains twists of thread, bits of lace, trimmings, fabric, and pins for knitting needles. For mother's embroidery, stretch and stick a scrap of fabric over a small button. Cut a narrow strip of paper, and stick it round the edge of the fabric-covered button to make the embroidery frame. Work a few stitches on the fabric within the frame using coloured thread.

Father

Cut off the curved ends of the peg as shown by the line marked B in the illustration, making the peg about 10 cm (4 in.) in length.

For the trousers use black felt. Cut a 4 cm by 6 cm ($1\frac{1}{2}$ in. by $2\frac{3}{8}$ in.) strip for each leg. Wrap a strip around each leg, overlapping and gluing the 6 cm ($2\frac{3}{8}$ in.) edges. Stick the top edges of the pants to the peg to hold them in place. Cut father's shoe piece from thin card, using the pattern given in diagram 12. Colour the shoe piece black, then stick it under the ends of the peg as shown on the pattern.

Mark on father's face, moustache and side whiskers as shown in the illustration. Glue strands of sewing thread all over the head for hair.

Make father's arms and shirt in the same way as for mother's blouse, but omit the lace trimming at the neck and wrists and, instead, stick round very narrow strips of fabric for collar and cuffs. Glue a scrap of ribbon at the shirt neck for a tie.

For the waistcoat use felt or thin fabric. To stop woven fabric fraying when cutting out, first spread the wrong side of the fabric with a thin coat of adhesive and allow it to dry. Cut out the waistcoat using the pattern given in diagram 13. Stick the waistcoat in place joining the shoulder edges on the shoulders and lapping the left front edge over the right front edge. Glue two rows of tiny beads down the waistcoat front for buttons.

Baby

Cut the peg in the same way as for mother. The top of the peg should now be sandpapered down to make the baby's head a little smaller than the adult dolls' heads.

Mark on the baby's face and a little hair on the forehead. Cover the remainder of the head by sticking on a scrap of lace for a bonnet. For the

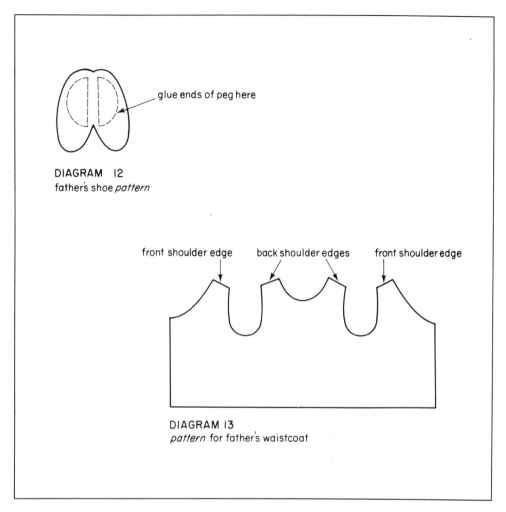

glue ends of peg here

DIAGRAM 12
father's shoe *pattern*

front shoulder edge   back shoulder edges   front shoulder edge

DIAGRAM 13
pattern for father's waistcoat

nightgown gather up a bit of trimming round the neck to just cover the peg.

Make the arms from a 6 cm (2⅜ in.) length of pipe cleaner, bending round a tiny bit at each end for the hands. Smooth the pipe cleaner hands to shape, spreading them with a little adhesive. Cover the arms with a strip of fabric formed into a tube in the same way as for mother, then glue the arms in position.

The Flexible Dolls

The father in illustration 38 is made from three pipe cleaners, and a wooden bead about 13 mm ($\frac{1}{2}$ in.) in diameter for the head. In illustration 39 the female dolls are made from pegs by the method already described in chapter 14. The cook, or nanny, is plainly dressed but the maid-servant and mother are fashionably dressed in the style of the 1890s.

To make the flexible doll

For the body and legs, glue two pipe cleaners into the wooden bead. Twist the pipe cleaners together for 3 cm ($1\frac{1}{8}$ in.), forming the body. Bend back the ends of the pipe cleaners 5 cm (2 in.), and twist along the legs, then bend up 1 cm ($\frac{3}{8}$ in.) at the end of each leg for the feet. Make the arms and cover the hands in exactly the same way as given for the peg dolls.

This makes a figure about the same size as the peg dolls, so that a mixture of both methods can be used if desired when making the family and servants.

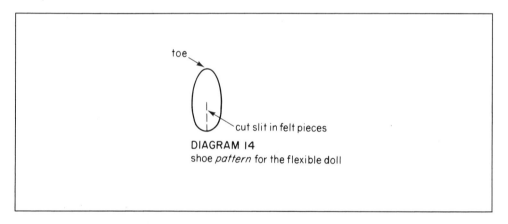

DIAGRAM 14
shoe *pattern* for the flexible doll

For the shoes, cut the shoe soles from thin card, using the pattern given in diagram 14. Cut the shoe uppers from felt, using the same pattern, then cut slits in the felt as shown by the dotted line on the pattern. Stick the soles under the feet, then stick the uppers in place, sandwiching the pipe cleaner feet between them. Stick the felt on either side of the slits around the pipe cleaner legs towards the back of the feet.

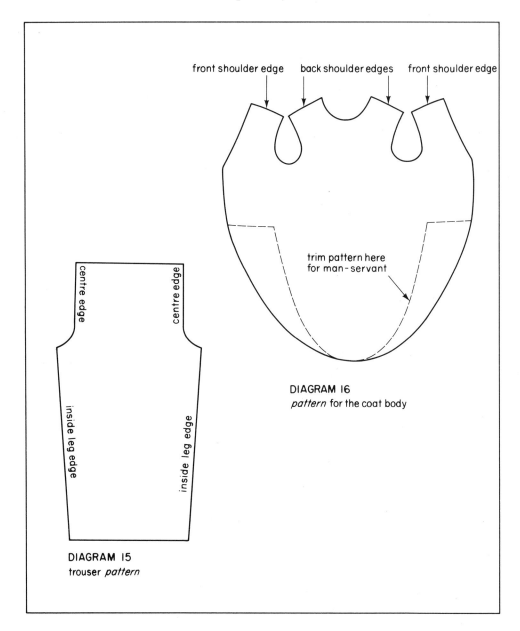

front shoulder edge   back shoulder edges   front shoulder edge

trim pattern here
for man-servant

DIAGRAM 16
pattern for the coat body

centre edge   centre edge

inside leg edge   inside leg edge

DIAGRAM 15
trouser *pattern*

Now wrap a little cotton wool around the body to pad it out slightly, tying the cotton wool in place with thread. Illustration 38 shows a partly-made doll with one hand covered on the arms piece and one foot complete with shoe. The cotton wool padding is also shown in position.

Father

Make a pipe cleaner doll, then mark the face and stick on the hair as given for the peg doll. Cut two trouser pieces from black or grey felt using the pattern shown in diagram 15. Join the pieces together at the centre edges by oversewing neatly. Bring these seams together and oversew the inside leg edges of each leg. Turn the trousers right side out. Put the trousers on the doll, then sew the waist edge to the cotton wool padding.

Stick a narrow strip of fabric around the neck for the shirt collar and a scrap of ribbon at the front of the collar for a tie.

For the coat sleeves cut a 2·5 cm by 11 cm (1 in. by $4\frac{1}{4}$ in.) strip of black felt. Oversew the long edges together, then slip the arms inside the sleeves,

having the hands protruding at each end. Sew the centre of the arms piece to the cotton wool at the back of the doll just below the neck.

Cut the coat body from black felt using the pattern shown in diagram 16. Put the coat on the doll, then lap and stick the front shoulder edges over the back shoulder edges. Lap the left front edge of the coat a little over the right front edge and stick in place, then stick on three tiny beads for buttons. Cut the collar from black felt using the pattern shown in diagram 17. Stick the collar round the neck of the coat.

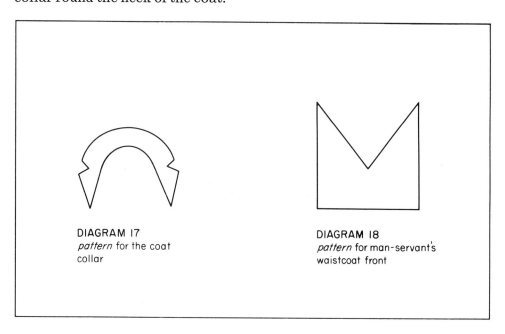

DIAGRAM 17
pattern for the coat
collar

DIAGRAM 18
pattern for man-servant's
waistcoat front

Man-servant
Make the trousers as for father. Stick a piece of white fabric to the doll's chest below the chin for the shirt front, then stick on the collar as for father. Make a small bow-shape from a scrap of ribbon for a tie, and stick it to the collar.

Cut the waistcoat front piece from white felt, using the pattern given in diagram 18, then stick this in place just lapping the lower edge over the top edge of the trousers. Stick on a few tiny beads for buttons.

Now make the arms, sleeves and coat as for father, noting that the fronts of the coat should be trimmed along the lines shown on the pattern.

Cook or nanny

Make as for the mother peg doll, wrapping a little cotton wool round the peg to make a plumper figure. Use plain, finely striped or checked fabric for the blouse and skirt to make a dress. Omit the lace cap and shoulder pieces described on mother's blouse. Note that the strip of fabric glued round the peg will be a little larger for this doll because of the cotton wool padding. Take in the extra fullness round the neck edge of the fabric by running round a gathering thread.

The mob cap is a 3·5 cm (1$\frac{3}{8}$ in.) diameter circle of fabric. Before cutting it out, stick a piece of white paper tissue to the wrong side of the fabric; this will stop the edges from fraying. Gather round the cap about 3 mm ($\frac{1}{8}$ in.) from the edge, and put it on the doll's head, pulling up the gathers to fit. Stick the cap in position.

For the apron bib, cut a 2 cm ($\frac{3}{4}$ in.) square of white fabric. Turn in three edges a little and stick down to neaten. Stick the bib to the front of the doll having the raw edge lapping the top edge of the skirt. Now stick narrow strips of ribbon up each side of the bib, over the shoulders to the back waist, crossing them over at the back.

Cut a 6 cm by 12 cm (2$\frac{3}{8}$ in. by 4$\frac{3}{4}$ in.) piece of white fabric for the apron. Turn in and stick all edges to neaten except for one 12 cm (4$\frac{3}{4}$ in.) edge. Gather this edge and glue it round the doll's waist, then stick on a strip of ribbon for the waistband to cover the gathered raw edges.

Maid-servant

The maid-servant wears a black dress with white cap and apron. Make the maid's bodice in the same way as for the mother peg doll. For the sleeves wrap a 3 cm by 10 cm (1$\frac{1}{8}$ in. by 4 in.) strip of fabric around the pipe cleaner arms piece to make close-fitting sleeves, and stick the long edge in place. Glue the arms in position. For the puffs at the tops of the sleeves, cut two 3 cm by 7 cm (1$\frac{1}{8}$ in. by 2$\frac{3}{4}$ in.) strips of fabric. Overlap and glue the short edges of each piece, then slip them in position on the doll. Turn in the remaining raw edges a little, run round gathering threads, then pull up the gathers and fasten off.

Make the apron in the same basic way as for the cook's apron, but use bits of lace trimming as shown in illustration 40. Gather up a bit of lace edging for the cap and stick to the front of the head then glue a bit of very narrow ribbon round the cap, tying it in place at the back.

Mother

Mother's dress is made in a similar way to the maid's with the addition of a few frills of ribbon and lace. Two fabrics, one plain and one patterned, in toning colours are used. For the dress skirt insert a strip of the patterned fabric at the front as shown in illustration 41. When gathering the skirt round the doll's waist, take most of the fullness to the back. Glue lace edging round the neck and wrists and a frill of lace at each side of the waist. Stick a strip of narrow ribbon round the waist ending in a bow at the back, then stick a frill of ribbon and a little lace edging over each shoulder.

CHAPTER SIXTEEN

The Milliner's Shop

Instead of constructing a whole dolls' house, a one-room setting can be very quickly made from a small box. Remove the top and front, leaving walls on only three sides and a floor. The furnishings of the room can be easily changed from bedroom to sitting-room, or from kitchen to nursery.

Most attractive miniature shops can also be made in the same way. Illustration 42 shows the fashionable mother doll choosing a new hat at the milliner's shop. The counter is made from an after-dinner mints box in the same way as the cupboard in chapter 8.

The hat stands are made from plastic golf markers and cocktail sticks. Cut most of the spike off the golf marker, then push the cocktail stick into the remaining small hole at the centre of the marker. Cut the hat stands to various heights as shown in the illustration, then paint them gold.

The curled feathers displayed around the shop are fronds cut off marabou dress trimming, or any other kinds of feathers which are available. To curl the feathers, draw them gently between a blunt knife blade and the thumb.

The pretty hats of the 1890s are made from circles of thin card about 2 cm ($\frac{3}{4}$ in.) in diameter, or strips of ribbon gathered into flat rosettes about the

same size. The trimmings are then piled up all over the hats. Glue them in place, positioning them with tweezers. For trimmings use looped or gathered ribbons, feathers, ribbon bows, dried flowers, grasses, and fabric flowers.

CHAPTER SEVENTEEN

The Market Stall

A miniature market stall is another easy-to-make idea for displaying a selection of miniature objects. Thin card is used for the base of the stall, the upright posts and cross pieces are made from 3 mm by 6 mm ($\frac{1}{8}$ in. by $\frac{1}{4}$ in.) strips of balsa wood. Balsa can be very easily cut with a craft knife or even scissors. If desired, strips of card may be used instead of balsa, gluing several layers together if necessary to give the required thickness.

Draw the shape shown in diagram 19 onto thin card then cut it out. Use the blade of a penknife held against a ruler to lightly score along the dotted lines shown on the pattern. Bend the card back along all the scored lines thus forming the box shape, then tuck under and glue the flaps in place as shown on the pattern.

For the posts at the corners of the stall cut four 14 cm ($5\frac{1}{2}$ in.) lengths of balsa. Glue them in position at the sides of the stall. For each of the cross pieces cut an 11 cm ($4\frac{1}{4}$ in.) length and stick in place 1 cm ($\frac{3}{8}$ in.) down from the top of the upright corner posts as shown in illustration 43.

For the cover around the sides of the stall cut a 7 cm ($2\frac{3}{4}$ in.) wide strip of cream-coloured cotton fabric, long enough to go all round the stall plus a

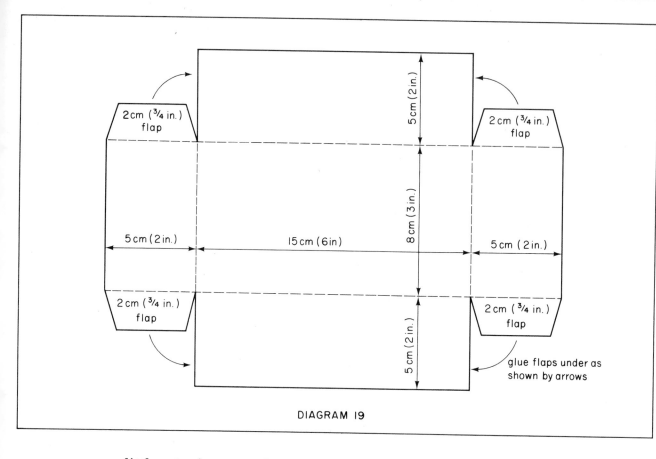

2cm (¾ in.) flap

2cm (¾ in.) flap

5cm (2in.)

5cm (2in.)

15cm (6in)

5cm (2in.)

5cm (2in.)

8cm (3in.)

5cm (2in.)

2cm (¾ in.) flap

2cm (¾ in.) flap

glue flaps under as shown by arrows

DIAGRAM 19

little extra for an overlap. Turn in the long raw edges of the strip 1 cm ($\frac{3}{8}$ in.) and stick down. Glue one long edge of the strip all round the stall having the other long edge touching the ground.

To cover the flat top of the stall cut a 14 cm by 17 cm ($5\frac{1}{2}$ in. by $6\frac{3}{4}$ in.) piece of white cotton fabric. Turn in all the raw edges 1 cm ($\frac{3}{8}$ in.) and stick down. Glue the strip across the top of the stall having the 17 cm ($6\frac{3}{4}$ in.) edges hanging down evenly at the front and back as shown in illustration 43.

To make the canvas awning which covers the top of the stall cut at 15 cm by 18 cm (6 in. by 7 in.) rectangle of stiff paper. Cut a piece of fawn-coloured cotton fabric 1 cm ($\frac{3}{8}$ in.) larger all round than the paper rectangle. Place the paper in the centre of the piece of fabric then fold over the 1 cm ($\frac{3}{8}$ in.) extra fabric onto the paper and stick down.

To make the apex shape on the awning, fold it in half having the fold parallel to the 18 cm (7 in.) edges. Now fold in the 15 cm (6 in.) edges a little

less than 1 cm ($\frac{3}{8}$ in.). Snip these folded-in portions where the apex fold crosses them. The completed awning, ready for fixing in place is shown in illustration 43. Place the awning in position over the stall as shown on the finished stall in illustration 43 and stick it in place where it touches the balsa cross pieces.

CHAPTER EIGHTEEN

The Fabric Stall

For the cardboard strips at the centre of each bolt of fabric cut rectangles of thin card measuring 1·5 cm by 4 cm ($\frac{5}{8}$ in. by 1$\frac{1}{2}$ in.). Use either plain fabrics or fabrics printed with the smallest possible designs. Note that lengths of 4 cm (1$\frac{1}{2}$ in.) wide ribbon can also be used. In order to have no raw edges showing on the bolts of fabric cut 8 cm (3 in.) widths about 18 cm (7 in.) in length. Fold in the long raw edges and press, to make a strip 4 cm (1$\frac{1}{2}$ in.) wide. Wrap the length of fabric around the card strip using dabs of glue to hold in place. A few lengths of fabric may be draped over the cross pieces of the stall if desired as shown in illustration 44.

For the box of ribbons and trimmings use a matchbox tray cut down to about 5 mm ($\frac{1}{4}$ in.) in depth or make a tiny box shape in the same basic way as the base of the stall. Cut 5 mm by 2 cm ($\frac{1}{4}$ in. by $\frac{3}{4}$ in.) strips of thin card then wind and stick narrow ribbon and lace trimming around them. For the box of assorted loose buttons, make a tiny card box, spread the base with glue then sprinkle on the smallest available beads. For the buttons on cards use tweezers to stick tiny beads onto strips of card.

For the yard-stick use a wooden cocktail stick. Snip off the pointed ends of the stick then make marks with pencil at even intervals around the stick dividing it into eighths.

Cut several 5 cm (2 in.) squares of brown wrapping paper then use a needle to take a thread through one corner of all the squares. Knot the thread. Bend a short piece of thick fuse wire into an 'S' shape for a hook, place this over one of the cross pieces then hang up the wrapping paper.

For the baskets in front of the stall which contain fabric remnants use thick cotton lace edging in a fawn or cream colour. Illustration 43 shows a piece of the type of lace which is suitable for making miniature baskets. The open-work portion of the lace can be cut away; only the more solid portion is used. Cut a 3 cm (1$\frac{1}{4}$ in.) diameter circle of card for the base of each basket. Glue the strip of lace round the edge of the base turning and sticking a small amount underneath the card. The basket should be about 2·5 cm (1 in.) deep. For the handles use a suitable bit cut off the lace edging or pull out a few threads and twist them together before sticking in place on the basket. Fill the baskets with tiny folded pieces of fabric as shown in the illustrations.

CHAPTER NINETEEN

The Country Produce Stall

All the items shown on the stall in illustrations 45 and 46 are made from self-hardening modelling clay. They should be left to dry after modelling then painted with enamel paints in the appropriate colours.

For the smallest plant pot use a pea-sized ball of clay. Press the ball onto a pencil point to make a hole in the centre and also to form the required tapered shape. Remove the shape and flatten the base of the plant pot. Use slightly larger balls of clay for the larger plant pots. After painting, fill the pots with dried flowers, sticking them in place.

For the centre of each lettuce roll a pea-sized ball of clay. Take small pinches of clay and flatten between finger and thumb then stick these 'leaves' around the lettuce centre. Curl back the outer leaves slightly. Make a small card box or use a matchbox tray to put the lettuces in.

Use a 6 cm by 14 cm ($2\frac{1}{4}$ in. by $5\frac{1}{2}$ in.) piece of brownish cotton fabric for the potato sack. Fold the piece bringing the 6 cm ($2\frac{1}{4}$ in.) edges together then take a narrow seam down each side. Turn the sack right side out and roll down the top. Fill the lower half of the sack with lumps of Plasticine then model a few uneven shapes for the potatoes making the medium ones about the size of a pea. Dot the potatoes lightly with a pencil point for the 'eyes'.

For the roast ham, roll a 2 cm ($\frac{3}{4}$ in.) diameter ball of clay then form into the tapered shape as shown in the illustration. Flatten the wide end as shown.

Roll a 2 cm ($\frac{3}{4}$ in.) diameter ball of clay for the cheese then flatten it to make the required shape. Use a craft knife to carefully cut out a couple of wedges before putting aside to dry.

Use a ball of clay a little larger than a pea for each pork pie. Form into a shape similar to the cheese, make a small hole in the top and also mark all round the top edge with a pencil point.

Form long tapered shapes for the crusty loaves measuring about 2·5 cm by 1 cm (1 in. by $\frac{3}{8}$ in.). Make cuts at intervals across the top. For the plaited loaves roll out thin snakes of clay and plait them, making the finished loaves about the same size as the crusty loaves. Make the cob loaves with a ball of clay at the bottom and a smaller one at the top.

46

For the various buns on the stall roll small balls of clay and flatten them. Make the eggs from tiny balls of clay and put them in a small basket made from lace edging as described for the baskets on the fabric stall.

Hang pieces of tissue paper on the stall instead of brown paper as described for the fabric stall.

The Street Vendor Doll

47

Make the peg doll in the same way as described for the mother peg doll in section 14 but do not cut off the end of the peg. Embed the end of the peg in a lump of Plasticine or clay so that the doll will not fall over when carrying a basket of wares.

Make a plain blouse and skirt and add an apron. For the hat use a 2·5 cm (1 in.) diameter circle of card and cut out the centre so that the hat will fit on top of the doll's head. Cover the hat with fabric and add a little decoration taking care to keep it fairly plain.

For the shawl cut a 12 cm ($4\frac{3}{4}$ in.) square of fabric. Fray out all the raw edges to make a fringe, then fold the shawl corner to corner and arrange around the doll as shown in illustration 47.

Make a basket in the same way as for the remnant baskets beside the fabric stall but not quite so deep. Make a handle which goes right over the top of the basket.

The basket may be filled with any of the items off the country produce stall. Alternatively it could be filled with oranges, apples, strawberries or bunches of tiny dried flowers to make a flower-seller doll.

List of Suppliers

Britain

W Hobby Ltd
62 Norwood High Street
London SE27 9NW
*dolls' house brick and slate paper and
acetate film*

The Needlewoman Shop
146 Regent Street
London W1
fabric and threads

Distinctive Trimmings & Co Ltd
11 Marylebone Lane
London W1
braids and trimmings

Paperchase Ltd
216 Tottenham Court Road
London W1
paper and card

USA

Yarncrafts Limited
3146 M Street
North West
Washington DC
fabrics and threads

Economy Handicrafts Inc
50–21 69th Street
Woodside, NY 11377
beads, paints, modelling clay

The Morilla Company Inc
43 21st Street
Long Island City, New York
paper and card

Bibliography

The Golden Age of Shop Design, edited by Alexandra Artley (Architectural Press).

The World of Victoriana, James Norbury (Hamlyn).

Antiques from the Victorian Home, Bea Howe (Batsford).

Victorian Comfort, John Gloag (David and Charles).

A History of Dolls' Houses, Flora Gill Jacobs (Cassell and Co. Ltd.).

Kitchen Antiques, Mary Norwak (Ward Lock).

Nursery Antiques, James Mackay (Ward Lock).